PSALMS

PRAYERS OF
THE HEART

EUGENE H.
PETERSON

12 STUDIES
FOR INDIVIDUALS
OR GROUPS

Life
Builder
Study

INTER-VARSITY PRESS
36 Causton Street, London SW1P 4ST, England
Email: ivp@ivpbooks.com
Website: www.ivpbooks.com

Originally published in the United States of America in the LifeGuide® Bible Studies series in 1987 by InterVarsity Press, Downers Grove, Illinois
Second edition published 2000
First published in Great Britain by Scripture Union in 1999
This edition published in Great Britain by Inter-Varsity Press 2018

British Library Cataloguing-in-Publication Data
A catalogue record for this book is available from the British Library.

ISBN: 978–1–78359–792–5

Printed in Great Britain by Ashford Colour Press Ltd, Gosport, Hampshire

Inter-Varsity Press publishes Christian books that are true to the Bible and that communicate the gospel, develop discipleship and strengthen the church for its mission in the world.

IVP originated within the Inter-Varsity Fellowship, now the Universities and Colleges Christian Fellowship, a student movement connecting Christian Unions in universities and colleges throughout Great Britain, and a member movement of the International Fellowship of Evangelical Students. Website: www.uccf.org.uk. That historic association is maintained, and all senior IVP staff and committee members subscribe to the UCCF Basis of Faith.

Contents

Getting the Most Out of *Psalms*

People look into mirrors to see how they look; they look into the Psalms to find out who they are. A mirror is an excellent way to learn about our appearance; the Psalms are the biblical way to discover ourselves. With a mirror we detect a new wrinkle here, an old wart there. We use a mirror when shaving or applying makeup to improve, if we can, the face we present to the world. With the psalms we bring into awareness an ancient sorrow, release a latent joy. We use the Psalms to present ourselves before God as honestly and thoroughly as we are able. A mirror shows us the shape of our nose and the curve of our chin, things we otherwise know only through the reports of others. The Psalms show us the shape of our souls and the curve of our sin, realities deep within us, hidden and obscured, for which we need focus and names.

Psalms: Poetry and Prayer

The Psalms are poetry and the Psalms are prayer. These two features need to be kept in mind always. If either is forgotten, the Psalms will not only be misunderstood but misused.

Poetry is language used with intensity. It is not, as so many suppose, decorative speech. Poets tell us what our eyes, blurred with too much gawking, and our ears, dulled with too much chatter, miss around and within us. Poets use words to drag us into the depths of reality itself, not by reporting on how life is but by pushing-pulling us into the middle of it. Poetry gets at the heart of existence. Far from being cosmetic language, it is intestinal. It is root language. Poetry doesn't so much tell us something we never knew as bring into recognition what was latent or forgotten or overlooked. The Psalms are almost entirely this kind of language. Knowing this, we will not be looking primarily for ideas about God in the Psalms or for direction in moral conduct. We will expect, rather, to find exposed and sharpened what it means to be human beings before God.

Prayer is language used in relation to God. It gives utterance to what we sense or want or respond to before God. God speaks to us; our answers are our prayers. The answers are not always articulate. Silence, sighs, groaning—these also constitute responses. But God is always involved, whether in darkness or light, whether in faith or despair. This is hard to get used to. Our habit is to talk *about* God, not *to* him. We love discussing God. But the Psalms resist such discussions. They are provided not to teach us about God but to train us in responding to him. We don't learn the Psalms until we are praying them.

Those two features, the poetry and the prayer, account for both the excitement and the difficulty in studying the Psalms. The *poetry* requires that we deal with our actual humanity—these words dive beneath the surfaces of pose and pretense straight into the depths. We are more comfortable with prose, the laid-back language of our ordinary discourse. The *prayer* requires that we deal with God—this God who is determined on nothing less than the total renovation of our lives. We would rather have a religious bull session.

One editorial feature of the Psalms helps to keep these distinctive qualities before us. The Psalms are arranged into five books. At the end of Psalm 41, 72, 89, 106 and 150, formula sentences indicate a conclusion. Because of these mini-conclusions the Psalms are usually printed (in English translations) as Book I (Psalm 1—41), Book II (42—72), Book III (73—89), Book IV (90—106) and Book V (107—150).

This five-book arrangement matches the five-book beginning of the Bible, deeply embedded in our minds as the five books of Moses. The five books of Moses are matched by the five books of David like two five-fingered hands clasping one another in greeting. In the five books of Moses God addresses us by his word, calling us into being and shaping our salvation. In the five books of David we personally respond to this word that addresses us.

Answering God

Prayer is answering speech. God's Word has not done its complete work until it evokes an answer from us. All our answers are prayers. The Psalms train us in this answering speech, this language that responds to all God's creating and saving words targeted to our lives.

Our usual approach to God's Word is to ask, What is God saying to me? That is almost always the correct question when reading Scripture. But in the Psalms the question is, How do I answer the God who speaks to me?

In the Psalms we do not primarily learn what God *says* to us but how to honestly, devoutly and faithfully *answer* his words to us. In the course of acquiring language we learn how to answer our parents, our teachers, our employers and our friends, but we do not get very much practice in answering God. The Psalms train us in answering God. And so we bring a somewhat different mindset to the Psalms than we do to the rest of Scripture—we are learning to *pray,* not study, although the two activities will always be interconnected.

We know almost nothing of the circumstances in which the 150 psalms were written. David is the most-named author, but most are anonymous. But that hardly matters, for the life-settings of the Psalms are not geographical or cultural but *interior.* Calvin called them "an anatomy of all the parts of the soul."

Everything that anyone can feel or experience in relation to God is in these prayers. You will find them the best place in Scripture to explore all the parts of your life and then to say who you are and what is in you—guilt, anger, salvation, praise—to the God who loves, judges and saves you in Jesus Christ. These twelve studies are designed to guide you into twelve interior dimensions of your life and bring them to expression before God.

Suggestions for Individual Study

1. As you begin each study, pray that God will speak to you through his Word.

2. Read the introduction to the study and respond to the personal reflection question or exercise. This is designed to help you focus on God and on the theme of the study.

3. Each study deals with a particular passage—so that you can delve into the author's meaning in that context. Read and reread the passage to be studied. If you are studying a book, it will be helpful to read through the entire book prior to the first study. The questions are written using the language of the New International Version, so you may wish to use that version of the Bible. The New Revised Standard Version is also recommended.

4. This is an inductive Bible study, designed to help you discover for yourself what Scripture is saying. The study includes three types of questions. *Observation* questions ask about the basic facts: who, what, when, where and how. *Interpretation* questions delve into the meaning of the passage. *Application* questions help you discover the implications of the text for growing in Christ. These three keys unlock the treasures of Scripture.

Write your answers to the questions in the spaces provided or in a personal journal. Writing can bring clarity and deeper understanding of yourself and of God's Word.

5. It might be good to have a Bible dictionary handy. Use it to look up any unfamiliar words, names or places.

6. Use the prayer suggestion to guide you in thanking God for what you have learned and to pray about the applications that have come to mind.

7. You may want to go on to the suggestion under "Now or Later," or you may want to use that idea for your next study.

Suggestions for Members of a Group Study

1. Come to the study prepared. Follow the suggestions for individual study mentioned above. You will find that careful preparation will greatly enrich your time spent in group discussion.

2. Be willing to participate in the discussion. The leader of your group will not be lecturing. Instead, he or she will be encouraging the members of the group to discuss what they have learned. The leader will be asking the questions that are found in this guide.

3. Stick to the topic being discussed. Your answers should be based on the verses which are the focus of the discussion and not on outside authorities such as commentaries or speakers. These studies focus on a particular passage of Scripture. Only rarely should you refer to other portions of the Bible. This allows for everyone to participate in in-depth study on equal ground.

4. Be sensitive to the other members of the group. Listen attentively when they describe what they have learned. You may be surprised by their insights! Each question assumes a variety of answers. Many questions do not have "right" answers, particularly questions that aim at meaning or application. Instead the questions push us to explore the passage more thoroughly.

When possible, link what you say to the comments of others. Also, be affirming whenever you can. This will encourage some of the more hesitant members of the group to participate.

5. Be careful not to dominate the discussion. We are sometimes so eager to express our thoughts that we leave too little opportunity for others to respond. By all means participate! But allow others to also.

6. Expect God to teach you through the passage being discussed and through the other members of the group. Pray that you will have an enjoyable and profitable time together, but also that as a result of the study you will find ways that you can take action individually and/or as a group.

7. Remember that anything said in the group is considered confidential and should not be discussed outside the group unless specific permission is given to do so.

8. If you are the group leader, you will find additional suggestions at the back of the guide.

1

Praying Our Inattention

Psalm 1

Family responsibilities. Work deadlines. Education goals. Home maintenance. So much is clamoring for our attention each day. And that's not to mention the distractions that come from the media. Most of us can't step immediately from the noisy high-stimulus world into the quiet concentration of prayer.

GROUP DISCUSSION. What thoughts and concerns most often distract when you begin to pray?

PERSONAL REFLECTION. Attempt to clear your mind before you begin to study. Sit in silence for a few moments. What thoughts and concerns come to mind? List them. Ask God to help you to focus on what he wants you to learn.

Psalm 1 is not prayer, exactly, but the preface to prayer. We do not begin to pray by praying but by coming to attention. Psalm 1 is the biblical preparation for a life of prayer. Step by step it detaches us from activities and words that distract us from God so that we can be attentive before him. Psalm 1 provides a kind of entryway into the place of prayer. *Read Psalm 1.*

1. What contrasts do you notice in the psalm?

2. The first word in the psalm is *blessed.* (Some translate it *happy.*) What kind of expectations should that bring to our life of prayer?

3. What significance do you see in the progression from *walk* to *stand* to *sit* (v. 1)?

4. "The law of the LORD" is contrasted with the words *counsel, way* and *seat.* What does this contrast bring out?

5. The psalmist describes the person who *delights* in God's law (v. 2). What is your emotional response to Scripture—not what you *believe* about it but how you *feel* about it?

6. *Tree* is the central metaphor of the psalm (v. 3). Put your imagination to use. How are law-delighting people like trees?

7. In what ways are the wicked like chaff (vv. 4-6)?

8. How do these two radically different portraits (the tree-righteous and the chaff-wicked) motivate you to delight in God's Word?

---

9. Do you feel a gap (or chasm!) between "real life" (work, school, family) and your prayer life? Explain.

---

10. How does meditation—listening to God speak to us through Scripture—prepare us for prayer?

---

11. How can you incorporate meditation on God's Word into your life?

---

12. Some prayer is spontaneous—a word of thanks, a cry of pain. Other prayer is routine—at meals, in public worship. But a *life* of prayer requires preparation, a procedure for moving from inattention to attention. The same *method* will not suit everyone. How can you develop an approach to meditation that fits your circumstances and development?

Ask God to help you keep your commitments to meditate and to pray.

Now or Later

Psalm 119 is an excellent passage to use in meditation. Use short chunks of it to reflect on as you prepare to pray this week.

2

Praying Our Intimidation

Psalm 2

We wake up each day in a world noisy with boasting, violent with guns, arrogant with money. How can we avoid being intimidated? What use can prayer have in the face of governments and armies and millionaires? None, if God is not at work; all, if God is.

GROUP DISCUSSION. Together, look at a handful of clippings from today's newspaper or this week's news magazine. What events in the world are particularly troubling to you and why?

PERSONAL REFLECTION. What bad news have you seen on the news or read in the paper lately? Pray about some of the events in the world that are troubling to you.

Psalm 2, like Psalm 1, is pre-prayer—an act of orientation that prepares us to pray. This psalm prepares us to pray in political as well as personal dimensions. God is as much at work in the public sphere as he is in the personal, and our prayers are as needful there as in our personal lives. *Read Psalm 2.*

1. What key nouns and verbs throughout the passage suggest the political orientation of this psalm?

2. Do you feel as responsible to pray for the nation, society and culture as you do for self, friends and church? Explain.

3. Compare the first verse of Psalm 1 to the last in Psalm 2. What do we learn from these two *blesseds?*

4. *Meditates* in Psalm 1:2 and *plot* in Psalm 2:1 are the same word in Hebrew. How is the word used differently in the two passages?

5. How does the Lord view the vaunted power of nations (vv. 4- 6)? How does this compare to or contrast with your attitude as you watch the evening news on television? Explain.

6. "Anointed One" in verse 2 is *Messiah* in Hebrew, *Christ* in Greek. What in this psalm reminds you of Jesus?

7. It has been traditional for Christians to pray this psalm on Easter Day. What in the psalm especially suits it for this occasion?

8. The psalm begins and ends with references to kings and rulers (vv. 2-3, 10-12). How do they relate to the King enthroned by the Lord (v. 6)?

What impact does this have on the way we pray?

9. It is always easier to pray for personal needs than political situations. But Psalm 2 is entirely political. Knowing this, what responsibility do we have as citizens of a particular country living in Christ's kingdom?

Pray for three rulers (presidents, kings, prime ministers or dictators) who you think are especially in need of God's guidance.

Now or Later

Spend time researching the life and work of one or more of the rulers you prayed for so that you can be more aware of how to continue to pray for them.

3

Praying Our Trouble

Prayer begins in a realization that we cannot help ourselves, so we must reach out to God. "Help!" is the basic prayer. We are in trouble, deep trouble. If God cannot get us out, we are lost; if God can get us out, we are saved. If we don't know that we need help, prayer will always be peripheral to our lives, a matter of mood and good manners. But the moment we know we are in trouble, prayer is a life-or-death matter.

GROUP DISCUSSION. What is the worst trouble you were in this last week? Where did you go for help? Did you get help?

PERSONAL REFLECTION. Recall a time when God has been your help. Thank him for coming through for you.

Psalm 3 is the first prayer in the Psalter. Psalms 1 and 2 prepared us for prayer; Psalm 3 prays. This psalm was written when David fled from his son Absalom, who was leading a rebellion against David. A huge battle ended with the death of twenty thousand. Then Absalom died: "He was riding his mule, and as the mule went out from under the thick branches of a large oak, Absalom's head got caught in the tree. He was left hanging in midair, while the mule he was riding kept on going" (2 Samuel 18:9). *Read Psalm 3.*

---

1. David's prayer naturally divides into five sections: verses 1-2, 3-4, 5-6, 7 and 8. Name each stanza with a single word or phrase.

---

2. What progression do you see from each section to the next?

---

3. David describes his foes in verses 1-2. Do you ever feel overwhelmed by threatening people or circumstances? Give an example.

---

4. *Deliver/deliverance* is a key word in this psalm. What do we learn about the nature of deliverance through its various uses here?

---

5. What actions is God described as taking in this psalm?

Are you used to thinking of God in these ways? Explain.

6. What actions is David described as taking in the psalm?

To what extent do these characterize you when trouble arises?

7. The emotional center of the psalm is verse 5. Take this seriously and ponder its significance. When we are sleeping, what are we doing?

What is God doing?

8. What kind of trouble are you in right now?

9. What in this psalm will help you to pray your trouble?

Talk to God about the things that are troubling you.

Now or Later

Take an image or phrase from Psalm 3 and use it to pray your trouble. Continue through the week.

4

Praying Our Creation

Psalm 8

Prayer is an orienting act. We begin to discover who we are when we realize where we are. Disorientation is a terrible experience. If we cannot locate our place, we are in confusion and anxiety. We are also in danger, for we are apt to act inappropriately. If we are among enemies and don't know it, we may lose our life. If we are among friends and don't know it, we may miss good relationships. If we are alongside a cliff and don't know it, we may lose our footing.

GROUP DISCUSSION. When traveling, have you ever awakened and not known where you were? The bed is unfamiliar; the room is strange; you don't recognize anything. What does it feel like to be disoriented?

PERSONAL REFLECTION. We find our way by focusing on God. How has God provided guidance in your life?

While praying Psalm 8, we find out where we are and some important aspects of who we are. *Read Psalm 8.*

---

1. Note the first and last sentences. What is the significance of these bracketing sentences for the psalm even before we know its contents?

2. Browse through the psalm and note every word that refers to what God has created. How do these things reveal God's glory?

3. How does Psalm 8 compare with the way you view yourself?

4. Why do you think the psalmist contrasts what children and infants say with what foes and avengers say in verse 2?

5. Bernard Lonergan once said that when an animal doesn't have anything to do, it goes to sleep; when humans don't have anything to do, they ask questions. What kind of question do we find at almost the exact center of this psalm (v. 4)?

What kind of answer is adequate to this question?

6. What evidence do we have that God cares for us?

7. Verse 5 comments on our *position* in creation. How does it contrast with positions we are put in by nonbiblical authorities?

_____

8. Verse 6 comments on our *responsibility* over creation. In what ways do you feel or not feel responsibility for your environment?

_____

9. The psalm lists six creatures (vv. 7-8) over which we have responsibility. Name six other items over which you accept responsibility.

_____

10. "Ruler" and "under his feet" (v. 6) can be twisted into excuses to exploit and pillage. What is there in this psalm to prevent such twisting?

_____

11. What adjustments do you need to make to view yourself as God views you?

The psalmist concludes as he began, with praise. Pray, praising God and using this psalm as the basis for your praise.

Now or Later

Let this psalm inspire you to enjoy God in creation. Get outdoors and pray your thanks to God for what you see around you.

5

Praying
Our Sin

Psalm 51

Alongside the basic fact that God made us good (Psalm 8) is the equally basic fact that we have gone wrong. We pray our sins to get to the truth about ourselves and to find out how God treats sinners. Our experience of sin does not consist in doing some bad things but in being bad. It is a fundamental condition of our existence, not a temporary lapse into error. Praying our sin isn't resolving not to sin anymore; it is discovering what God has resolved to do with us as sinners.

GROUP DISCUSSION. "Sin" has become an unpopular and little-used word in our culture. Why do you think this is?

PERSONAL REFLECTION. How honest are you about your sin? Rate yourself on a scale of 1 to 10. Why do you rate yourself in this way? The psalm title refers this prayer to David's adultery with Bathsheba (2 Samuel 11—12). *Read Psalm 51.*

---

1. How many different synonyms for sin are in David's prayer?

How do we describe what we dislike in ourselves?

What does this tell us about the nature of sin?

---

2. As Christians, we know we are sinful. Why then is it so painful to be confronted with a specific sin?

---

3. What is God asked to do about sin? (Count and name the verbs.)

---

4. If I have been a sinner from birth (v. 5), sin must be something more than doing wrong things. What else could it be?

---

5. Verses 1-9 exhibit a heightened awareness of sin. What do they make you aware of?

6. Verse 10 is the center sentence. How does it center the prayer?

7. What parallel does create have with Genesis 1:1?

8. Forgiveness is an internal action with external consequences. What are some of them (vv. 13-17)?

9. What do you understand a "broken and contrite heart" to be (v. 17)?

What is your experience of this condition?

10. According to verses 18-19, what is the relationship between personal forgiveness and social righteousness?

11. Psalm 51 makes us aware of how sinful we are, and it makes us less actively sinful. How do you see it working that way in you?

Be quiet before God. In silence confess your sins to him. Accept his forgiveness and grace.

Now or Later

Try writing a history of your sin. In *Praying the Scriptures* Evan Howard describes how to do this, adapting an exercise developed by Ignatius of Loyola.

> You begin by reading and rereading the story of the first sin, found in Genesis 3. Get a sense of the story's place and events. Ask the Lord to increase your awareness of sin and to give you appropriate sorrow for it. Then imagine the story taking place before you, watching it happen as though peeking from behind a bush. . . .
>
> Then write out a history of your own sin, starting at the beginning with the particular sin in question. As in the previous step, note the beginning, movements, acts and consequences of this sin. . . . If others had a bad influence on you, admit your hurt and forgive them. You may be unconscious of aspects of your sin, so feel free to ask the Lord to show them to you. Be thorough but not morbidly introspective. ([Downers Grove, Ill.: InterVarsity Press, 1999], p. 79.)

6

Praying Our Salvation

Psalm 103

What God has done for us far exceeds anything we have done for or against him. The summary word for this excessive, undeserved, unexpected act by God is *salvation*. Prayer explores the country of salvation, tramping the contours, smelling the flowers, touching the outcroppings. There is more to do than recognize the sheer fact of salvation and witness to it; there are unnumbered details of grace, of mercy, of blessing to be appreciated and savored. Prayer is the means by which we do this.

GROUP DISCUSSION. Think of one of the best things that ever happened to you. Describe some of the details of why it was so good.

PERSONAL REFLECTION. Spend some time journaling about your perfect day. What would you do? Where? Who would be with you? How would it feel?

Psalm 103 expresses the *experience* (not the doctrine) of salvation. This is what it *feels* like to be saved. *Read Psalm 103.*

---

1. What are your general impressions of the psalm?

2. Note the first and last sentences. How does this bracketing affect your understanding of the psalm's contents?

3. Salvation is more richly complex than we sometimes think. What five actions of God add up to salvation (vv. 3-5)?

4. Describe how you have benefitted from one or more of God's actions in verses 3-5.

5. How did God make his ways known to Moses and Israel (v. 7)?

6. What astounding statements about God does the psalmist make in verses 8-14?

Which ones in particular expand what is puny in your thinking?

7. Carefully observe the contrast between us (vv. 15-16) and God (vv. 17-19). Does this make you feel better or worse about yourself? Explain.

8. Praying our salvation concludes by praising the saving God. The praise is orchestrated in verses 20-22. Who are the players in this hierarchy of praises?

Who else would you like to call into the orchestra?

9. What does it mean for you to be saved?

10. What dimensions of salvation would you like to explore further?

If you are studying this psalm alone, add your personal notes of praise in a time of prayer. If you are studying this with a group, pray together now as a chamber orchestra, each contributing your own notes.

Now or Later

Write a psalm of praise—on your own or with a group. Freely use your own words—don't try to sound like the psalmist. Express the joys of your daily life and the world around you as you see God at work. It's fun to work with a group, passing around a sheet of paper and each contributing a line.

7

Praying
Our Fear

Psalm 23

The world is a fearsome place. If we manage with the help of parents, teachers and friends to survive the dangers of infancy and childhood, we find ourselves launched in an adult world that is ringed with terror—accident, assault, disease, violence, conflicts.

GROUP DISCUSSION. What are your recurring fears?

PERSONAL REFLECTION. Write about a fear you are struggling with. What are its roots? How would you like God to deal with it?

Prayer brings fear into focus and faces it. But prayer does more than bravely face fear, it affirms God's presence in it. *Read Psalm 23.*

1. This is a well-known psalm. It takes strenuous effort to see it in a fresh way. Is there anything here you have never noticed before?

2. There are two large metaphors in the psalm: the shepherd (vv. 1-4) and the host (vv. 5-6). Compare and contrast these two images.

3. Look carefully at the shepherd. How exactly does he care for his sheep (vv. 1-4)?

4. How does the setting of verse 4 contrast with that of verses 1-3?

5. "I fear no evil" (v. 4) is a bold statement. What does it mean for you to say that?

6. Look carefully at the host. How exactly does he provide for his guest (vv. 5-6)?

7. How many times does the first-person pronoun (*I, me, my,*) occur in this psalm?

What impact does this make on you?

8. Enemies are prominent in the psalm prayers and appear here. Who are your enemies?

9. What is the most comforting thing that you have experienced in the life of faith?

10. Psalm 23 is a weapon against fear. What fear in your life will you go to war against with this prayer as your cannon?

Pray. Name your fears and ask Christ the Shepherd and Christ the Host to relieve them.

Now or Later

Isaiah 40 is another passage that brings much comfort in times of fear. Read through it and make parts of it your prayer to God for strength and courage.

8

Praying
Our Hate

Psalm 137

We want to be at our best before God. Prayer, we think, means presenting ourselves before God so that he will be pleased with us. We put on our "Sunday best" in our prayers. But when we pray the prayers of God's people, the psalms, we find that will not do. We must pray who we actually are, not who we think we should be.

GROUP DISCUSSION. Everyone has hated at one time or another. Be honest. Whom have you hated? Why?

PERSONAL REFLECTION. How do you feel about yourself, your life and others when you experience hate?

Here is a prayer that brings out not the best but the worst in us: vile, venomous, vicious hate. Can God handle our hate? *Read Psalm 137.*

---

1. This psalm combines the loveliest lyric we can sing with the ugliest emotion we can feel. What makes verses 1-6 lovely?

What makes verses 7-9 ugly?

2. The Babylonian exile put God's people where they did not want to be, with no hope of returning. When have you been where you didn't want to be?

Do verses 1-3 express anything similar to your experience? Explain.

3. Remembering your own experiences, how would you evaluate the emotions described in verses 4-6?

4. Why was Israel in Babylon, and how does that factor into the feelings they are expressing?

5. Israelites were an oft-conquered, much-trampled people. The Edomites in the past (v. 7) and the Babylonians (v. 8) in the present were oppressors. Imagine what it would be like to be the world's patsy. How might that shape your prayers?

6. Notice again the change in tone in verses 7-9. What words and phrases reveal the emotions in these verses?

7. It is easy to be honest before God with our hallelujahs and in our hurt; it is not easy to be honest in the dark emotions of our hate. How honest are you? Explain.

8. Jesus said "Love your enemies and pray for those who persecute you" (Matthew 6:44). How can we possibly love and pray for such people?

9. The two dominant emotions in this prayer are self-pity (vv. 1-6) and avenging hate (vv. 7-9), neither of them particularly commendable. Praying our sins doesn't, as such, launder them. What does it do?

10. Most of us suppress our negative emotions (unless, neurotically, we advertise them). The way of prayer is not to cover them up so we will appear respectable but to expose them so we can be healed. What negative emotion would you like healed?

Take any hate or dislike that you have uncovered and give it voice as you pray.

Now or Later

Read Psalm 138 and 139 and continue to pray your hate and other strong emotions to the God who knows your thoughts.

9

Praying
Our Tears

Tears are a biological gift of God. They are a physical means for expressing emotional and spiritual experience. But it is hard to know what to do with them. If we indulge our tears, we cultivate self-pity. If we suppress our tears, we lose touch with our feelings.

GROUP DISCUSSION. What was the last movie that made you cry? Why?

PERSONAL REFLECTION. When was the last time you cried—*really cried?*

When we pray our tears, we enter into sadnesses that integrate our sorrows with our Lord's sorrows and discover both the source of and the relief from our sadness. *Read Psalm 6.*

1. What different emotions are expressed in this psalm?

2. It is not popular in our culture to talk of an angry God (v. 1). What

experience have you had of God's anger?

3. Compare the first verse with the last. Are the tears because of the Lord or the enemies? Explain.

4. "How long?" (v. 3) is a frequent question in prayer. Considering the frequency with which it is uttered in Scripture, God must welcome it. What in your life, past or present, evokes this question?

5. What is the cumulative effect of the three verbs *turn, deliver* and *save* in verse 4?

6. The emotional center of this prayer is verses 6-7. How many different ways is weeping expressed?

7. Why the tears? Go through the psalm and note every possible source.

8. Tears are often considered a sign that something is wrong with us—depression, unhappiness, frustration—and therefore either to be avoided or to be cured. But what if they are a sign of something right with us? What rightness could they be evidence of?

9. In verses 8-9 there are three phrases in parallel: *weeping, cry for mercy* and *prayer.* Are these aspects of one thing or three different things? Explain.

10. Remembering and praising (v. 5) are set forth as if they should mean something to God. Why should they?

Are you practiced and skilled in remembering and praising? Explain.

11. Who do you know who is in grief?

Pray for those who are in grief now, using phrases from Psalm 6 to express their sorrow.

Now or Later

If you are feeling sadness over something in your own life, find a private time and place to pour your feelings out to the God who accepts all of your emotions.

10

Praying
Our Doubt

Doubt is not a sin. It is an essential element in belief. Doubt is honesty. Things are not as they appear. We see contradictions between what we believe and what we experience. What is going on here? Did God give us a bum steer? Why aren't things turning out the way we were taught to expect? No mature faith avoids or denies doubt. Doubt forces faith to bedrock.

GROUP DISCUSSION. What doubts have you had or do you have about the Christian life?

Do you feel guilty about expressing such doubts? Why?

PERSONAL REFLECTION. In a time of quiet ask yourself what doubts might be standing between you and God. Talk to God about those doubts.

The writer of Psalm 73 is full of doubt. *Read Psalm 73.*

1. How would you paraphrase the doubt expressed in verses 2-12?

2. The questions the psalmist asks are very relevant to us. What individuals or groups of people cause you to ask these kinds of questions?

---

3. Self-pity is like a deadly virus. How would you express, in terms of your own life, what the psalmist says in verses 13-14?

---

4. The key word and the pivotal center of the psalm is the word *till* in verse 17. What takes place here in the sanctuary?

---

5. What takes place in your sanctuary, the place where you worship?

---

6. How do some of the psalmist's realizations and understandings come into focus in your act of worship?

---

7. The *yet* in verse 23 links two contrasting statements. What are they?

How have you experienced this truth?

8. The prosperity of the wicked occupied the first part of the psalm (vv. 1-16). The presence of the Lord occupies the second (vv. 17-28). What is more vivid to you, the wicked or the Lord? Explain.

9. The appearance of the wicked whom we envy is in utter and complete contrast to their reality (vv. 18-20). How do you discern between what you see (and are tempted to envy) and what is (and so are affirmed in obedience)?

10. Worship is the pivotal act in this prayer. How can worship help you to deal with your doubts and hard questions about the Christian life?

11. The Christian consensus about worship is that it is a pivotal act every week. How can worship become a more pivotal part of your experience?

In your time of prayer spend five minutes in silence, savoring God's presence, letting him restore your perspective. Then speak your praises.

Now or Later
Read Psalm 49 for another perspective on the fate of the wicked.

11

Praying
Our Death

We live in a society characterized by the denial of death. This is unusual. Most people who have lived on this earth have given a great deal of attention to death. Preparing for a good death has been, in every century except our own, an accepted goal in life.

GROUP DISCUSSION. When you think about your own death, what do you think about? What do you feel?

PERSONAL REFLECTION. What death has affected you most deeply?

Psalm 90 has been part of preparation for death for millions of Christians. *Read Psalm 90.*

---

1. What different pictures of God do you get throughout this passage?

---

2. Death sets a limit to our lives and stimulates reflection on the context of life, which is not death, but God. In verses 1-2, how does the psalmist set death within his view of God?

---

3. Review the basis of verse 3 in Genesis 2:7 and 3:17-19. How does the knowledge of your mortality affect the way you live your life?

---

4. Why would God be angry with you (vv. 7-9)?

---

5. How does the psalmist describe God's anger and its effects on our lives (vv. 7-11)?

---

6. How do you integrate this view of God with John's well-known statement "God is love"?

---

7. Luther commented on verse 12: "Lord, teach us all to be such arithmeticians!" What does it mean to number our days aright?

---

8. How long do you expect to live, and how many years more does that give you?

How do you plan to live the years left to you?

---

9. The psalmist's sense of mortality is dramatic (vv. 4-6). How do modern hospitals blunt this sense of brevity and fragility?

---

10. This prayer brings death into focus. But it does far more—it brings *God* into focus. Study the verbs in verses 14-17. What emerges as most important for you—the things that you do for the rest of your life or what God will do in your life? Explain.

---

11. Plato believed philosophy was nothing more than a study of death. In the Middle Ages pastoral care concentrated on preparing for a good death. How does meditation on death affect the way you live?

Pray your awareness that you will die. In your prayers be conscious of Christ's death.

Now or Later

What are the key things that you want others to notice in your life? Make a list of five or so key character qualities or values that you would like to live out.

12

Praying Our Praise

All prayer finally, in one way or another, becomes praise. No matter how much we suffer, no matter our doubts—everything finds its way into praise, the final consummating prayer. This is not to say that other prayers are inferior to praise, only that all prayer pursued far enough becomes praise.

GROUP DISCUSSION. On a piece of poster board or a large sheet of paper write about or draw the things you are thankful for. Have fun! Include the everyday joys of life as well as the big answers to prayer.

PERSONAL REFLECTION. What circumstances or feelings in the last year have, however momentarily, made a praising person out of you?

Psalm 150 is deliberately placed as the concluding prayer of the church's book of prayers. *Read Psalm 150.*

---

1. How many times is the word *praise* used in the psalm?

What does that suggest about the psalmist's mood when he was writing this?

When have you felt compelled to express your praise to God in a similar way?

_____

2. Verse 1 tells us where the Lord is to be praised. What is the meaning of "in his sanctuary" and "in his mighty heavens"?

_____

3. Verse 2 tells us *why* he is to be praised. What reasons does the psalmist give?

What reasons of your own can you add?

_____

4. Verses 3-5 tell us *how* to praise the Lord. As you read these verses, what kind of scene do you imagine?

How does this kind of worship compare with your own?

5. Verse 6 tells us *who* should praise the Lord. Do you think that "everything that has breath" is meant literally? Explain.

6. In Hebrew the first and last word of this prayer is *hallelujah* ("praise the Lord"). To what extent is your life bracketed by this word?

7. There are no shortcuts to praise. If we maintain a sensitivity to all the psalms preceding this one, we will not be insensitive to all the tears and doubts and pain that are summed up into praise. What difficult circumstances in your life have found their way into praise?

8. Augustine claimed that a "Christian should be a hallelujah from head to foot." Are you? Do you want to be? What needs to be done to get you there?

Pray your praise. Gather the reflections and insights that have come from your study and turn them into a time of concluding and celebrative praise.

Now or Later

Write a psalm of praise celebrating what you have learned from this study individually or corporately if you are studying with a group.

Leader's Notes

MY GRACE IS SUFFICIENT FOR YOU. (2 COR 12:9)

Leading a Bible discussion can be an enjoyable and rewarding experience. But it can also be *scary*—especially if you've never done it before. If this is your feeling, you're in good company. When God asked Moses to lead the Israelites out of Egypt, he replied, "O Lord, please send someone else to do it"! (Ex 4:13). It was the same with Solomon, Jeremiah and Timothy, but God helped these people in spite of their weaknesses, and he will help you as well.

You don't need to be an expert on the Bible or a trained teacher to lead a Bible discussion. The idea behind these inductive studies is that the leader guides group members to discover for themselves what the Bible has to say. This method of learning will allow group members to remember much more of what is said than a lecture would.

These studies are designed to be led easily. As a matter of fact, the flow of questions through the passage from observation to interpretation to application is so natural that you may feel that the studies lead themselves. This study guide is also flexible. You can use it with a variety of groups—student, professional, neighborhood or church groups. Each study takes forty-five to sixty minutes in a group setting.

There are some important facts to know about group dynamics and encouraging discussion. The suggestions listed below should enable you to effectively and enjoyably fulfill your role as leader.

Preparing for the Study

1. Ask God to help you understand and apply the passage in your own life. Unless this happens, you will not be prepared to lead others. Pray too for the various members of the group. Ask God to open your hearts

to the message of his Word and motivate you to action.

2. Read the introduction to the entire guide to get an overview of the entire book and the issues which will be explored.

3. As you begin each study, read and reread the assigned Bible passage to familiarize yourself with it.

4. This study guide is based on the New International Version of the Bible. It will help you and the group if you use this translation as the basis for your study and discussion.

5. Carefully work through each question in the study. Spend time in meditation and reflection as you consider how to respond.

6. Write your thoughts and responses in the space provided in the study guide. This will help you to express your understanding of the passage clearly.

7. It might help to have a Bible dictionary handy. Use it to look up any unfamiliar words, names or places. (For additional help on how to study a passage, see chapter five of *How to Lead a LifeBuilder Study*, IVP, 2018.)

8. Consider how you can apply the Scripture to your life. Remember that the group will follow your lead in responding to the studies. They will not go any deeper than you do.

9. Once you have finished your own study of the passage, familiarize yourself with the leader's notes for the study you are leading. These are designed to help you in several ways. First, they tell you the purpose the study guide author had in mind when writing the study. Take time to think through how the study questions work together to accomplish that purpose. Second, the notes provide you with additional background information or suggestions on group dynamics for various questions. This information can be useful when people have difficulty understanding or answering a question. Third, the leader's notes can alert you to potential problems you may encounter during the study.

10. If you wish to remind yourself of anything mentioned in the leader's notes, make a note to yourself below that question in the study.

Leading the Study

1. Begin the study on time. Open with prayer, asking God to help the group to understand and apply the passage.

2. Be sure that everyone in your group has a study guide. Encourage the group to prepare beforehand for each discussion by reading the introduction to the guide and by working through the questions in the study.

3. At the beginning of your first time together, explain that these studies are meant to be discussions, not lectures. Encourage the members of the group to participate. However, do not put pressure on those who may be hesitant to speak during the first few sessions. You may want to suggest the following guidelines to your group.

☐ Stick to the topic being discussed.

☐ Your responses should be based on the verses which are the focus of the discussion and not on outside authorities such as commentaries or speakers.

☐ These studies focus on a particular passage of Scripture. Only rarely should you refer to other portions of the Bible. This allows for everyone to participate in in-depth study on equal ground.

☐ Anything said in the group is considered confidential and will not be discussed outside the group unless specific permission is given to do so.

☐ We will listen attentively to each other and provide time for each person present to talk.

☐ We will pray for each other.

4. Have a group member read the introduction at the beginning of the discussion.

5. Every session begins with a group discussion question. The question or activity is meant to be used before the passage is read. The question introduces the theme of the study and encourages group members to begin to open up. Encourage as many members as possible to participate, and be ready to get the discussion going with your own response.

This section is designed to reveal where our thoughts or feelings need to be transformed by Scripture. That is why it is especially important not to read the passage before the discussion question is asked. The passage will tend to color the honest reactions people would otherwise give because they are, of course, supposed to think the way the Bible does.

You may want to supplement the group discussion question with an icebreaker to help people to get comfortable. See the community section of the *Small Group Starter Kit* (IVP, 1995) for more ideas.

You also might want to use the personal reflection question with your group. Either allow a time of silence for people to respond individually or discuss it together.

6. Have a group member (or members if the passage is long) read aloud the passage to be studied. Then give people several minutes to read the passage again silently so that they can take it all in.

7. Question 1 will generally be an overview question designed to briefly survey the passage. Encourage the group to look at the whole passage, but try to avoid getting sidetracked by questions or issues that will be addressed later in the study.

8. As you ask the questions, keep in mind that they are designed to be used just as they are written. You may simply read them aloud. Or you may prefer to express them in your own words.

There may be times when it is appropriate to deviate from the study guide. For example, a question may have already been answered. If so, move on to the next question. Or someone may raise an important question not covered in the guide. Take time to discuss it, but try to keep the group from going off on tangents.

9. Avoid answering your own questions. If necessary, repeat or rephrase them until they are clearly understood. Or point out something you read in the leader's notes to clarify the context or meaning. An eager group quickly becomes passive and silent if they think the leader will do most of the talking.

10. Don't be afraid of silence. People may need time to think about the question before formulating their answers.

11. Don't be content with just one answer. Ask, "What do the rest of you think?" or "Anything else?" until several people have given answers to the question.

12. Acknowledge all contributions. Try to be affirming whenever possible. Never reject an answer. If it is clearly off-base, ask, "Which verse led you to that conclusion?" or again, "What do the rest of you think?"

13. Don't expect every answer to be addressed to you, even though this will probably happen at first. As group members become more at ease, they will begin to truly interact with each other. This is one sign of healthy discussion.

14. Don't be afraid of controversy. It can be very stimulating. If you don't resolve an issue completely, don't be frustrated. Move on and keep it in mind for later. A subsequent study may solve the problem.

15. Periodically summarize what the group has said about the passage. This helps to draw together the various ideas mentioned and gives continuity to the study. But don't preach.

16. At the end of the Bible discussion you may want to allow group members a time of quiet to work on an idea under "Now or Later." Then discuss what you experienced. Or you may want to encourage group members to work on these ideas between meetings. Give an opportunity during the session for people to talk about what they are learning.

17. Conclude your time together with conversational prayer, adapting the prayer suggestion at the end of the study to your group. Ask for God's help in following through on the commitments you've made.

18. End on time.

Many more suggestions and helps are found in *How to Lead a LifeBuilder Study*.

Components of Small Groups

A healthy small group should do more than study the Bible. There are four components to consider as you structure your time together.

Nurture. Small groups help us to grow in our knowledge and love of God. Bible study is the key to making this happen and is the foundation of your small group.

Community. Small groups are a great place to develop deep friendships with other Christians. Allow time for informal interaction before and after each study. Plan activities and games that will help you get to know each other. Spend time having fun together—going on a picnic or cooking dinner together.

Worship and prayer. Your study will be enhanced by spending time praising God together in prayer or song. Pray for each other's needs—and keep track of how God is answering prayer in your group. Ask God to help you to apply what you are learning in your study.

Outreach. Reaching out to others can be a practical way of applying what you are learning, and it will keep your group from becoming self-focused. Host a series of evangelistic discussions for your friends or neighbors. Clean up the yard of an elderly friend. Serve at a soup kitchen together, or spend a day working in the community.

Many more suggestions and helps in each of these areas are found in the *Small Group Starter Kit*. You will also find information on building a small group. Reading through the starter kit will be worth your time.

Study 1. Psalm 1. Praying Our Inattention.

Purpose: To learn to prepare to pray.

General note. Much prayer flounders because there is no preparation for prayer. Our school of prayer, the psalms, takes adequate time to prepare us to pray. Prayer is the cultivation and exploration of our best in relationship with God. It is essential not to be in a hurry. Preparation needs to be leisurely.

Group discussion. These questions are placed at the beginning of each study to help the group warm up to each other and to get people thinking along the lines of the topic of study. It is important not to read the passage before the question is asked because giving honest responses to various issues before they find out what the Bible says may help people see where their thoughts or attitudes need to be changed.

Personal reflection. This question is designed for individuals studying alone. However, if you are leading a group, you may want to allow a few minutes of quiet for people to complete this exercise.

Question 3. If the group has trouble seeing the significance of this progression, point out that the verbs go from movement to nonmovement, ending up "set in your ways."

Question 4. We prepare to pray by weaning ourselves away from listening to what everybody in family and school and culture is saying to us, and attending to what *God* is saying to us.

Question 5. Prime the pump here with some negative responses. Many people feel bored, doubtful or bewildered when reading Scripture. These feelings need to be admitted and faced. If they are not admitted and dealt with, the "delight" will be forced and become a pose.

Question 7. Some people in the group may not know what chaff is. You might briefly explain that when grain is threshed the worthless part (the seed covering and other debris) separates from the valuable grain. Later, in an ancient process known as winnowing, the grain and chaff are thrown into the air. The wind blows away the chaff because it is light, but the heavier grain falls back to earth.

> Metaphorically, chaff pictures something not worth keeping, to be burned
> up by fire—whether God's enemies (Ex 15:7; Num 1:20) or apostate Israel
> (Is 5:24) or the faithful being sifted by Satan. This is the category of imag-
> ery John the Baptist uses when he speaks of Jesus with a winnowing fork in
> his hand to gather the wheat into the barn and to burn up the chaff . . . (Mt
> 3:12; Lk 3:17). (Leland Ryken et al., ed., *The Dictionary of Biblical Imagery*
> [Downers Grove, Ill.: InterVarsity Press, 1998], p. 136.)

Question 10. Christians have always seen prayer as one element in a
two-part rhythm: God speaks to us in Scripture; we answer him in prayer.
The slow, leisurely "listening-reading" of Scripture cannot be overempha-
sized as preparation for prayer.

Study 2. Psalm 2. Praying Our Intimidation.

Purpose: To prepare to pray by setting the world around us before the
lordship of God.

General note. Often we are intimidated by the world because it seems
intractable to the life of faith. So we reduce our prayers to private exer-
cises in personal virtue. We need to prepare for the practice of prayer as a
world power.

Group discussion. Come prepared with clippings, or prior to the study
ask each member to bring some clippings.

Question 2. Another way to ask this would be: "Do the news items discussed earlier motivate you to pray with the same level of urgency as
when you hear of a friend who has cancer or when you face a personal or
family crisis? Why or why not?"

Question 4. Meditation involves passionate attentiveness. It is not mere
daydreaming on your knees. Plotting against God is common enough in
the world, but is there an equivalent "plotting" in the church in consulta-
tion with God? Charles Williams says in his novel *All Hallows Eve* that a
"cruel purpose could outspeed a vague pity." Do you "plot/meditate" the
world's salvation as energetically as the politicians do their strategies?

Question 5. If the discussion flounders, point out that it is possible to
take the power of political evil too solemnly—to be too worried about it.
A gentle mockery might be more biblical.

Question 7. The resurrection is the triumph of God over the plot of powerful Rome and Israel against God's anointed.

Question 8. It is easy to restrict Christ's rule to the soul. Discuss the political dimensions that are explicit in Jesus (that is, his political *purposes* for people living together in peace and justice). You will need to be ready to distinguish this from political *means* of wars and legislatures.

Now or Later. Ask the members of the group to talk about one nation, other than our own, that they have a special interest in. Discuss the interest. Ask them to make a commitment during the course of this study to make daily intercessory prayer for that nation and its people, and to keep notes on how they feel about it.

As follow-up, you could spend a meeting just praying for the nations you have chosen. Have each member give a little background on the nation and leader they are praying for to guide you. *Operation World* is a great resource for this.

Study 3. Psalm 3. Praying Our Trouble.

Purpose: To probe for the place of need in our lives that evokes the cry for "help" to God, and to learn how to ask for God's help modeled by Psalm 3.

Background note. If you are unfamiliar with Absalom's conspiracy, you might want to read through 2 Samuel 15—18 to prepare for the study.

Group discussion. We are encouraged to be self-sufficient in our society. Asking for help is widely interpreted to be a sign of weakness. As a consequence much asking for help is done on the sly or not at all. Discuss how people feel about asking for help in this broader cultural atmosphere.

Question 3. It's easier to talk about threatening circumstances than threatening people. It isn't "nice" to admit that we have enemies. If necessary, remind the group that Jesus didn't say that we weren't supposed to have them, but rather that we were supposed to pray for them. A sharp-edged sense of "enemy" is essential to prayer.

Question 4. *Deliver* has several synonyms. The most familiar is *save*. Sometimes these words are reserved exclusively for reference to the soul's eternal salvation. Push the discussion outward, getting as much included in God's action as the imagination of the group can handle.

Question 5. Notice actions in verses 3, 4, 5, 7 (requested action) and 8.

Question 6. Notice actions in verses 4 and 5. Also in verse 7 we see the psalmist calling on God. In verse 8 the psalmist declares his faith that God will come through for him.

Questions 8-9. If you think people would be too intimidated to answer question 8 in front of the whole group, you might have them break into twos or threes to answer these questions; then pray for one another.

Prayer. Spend time praying for each other, as a group or in twos or threes, and carry a list away from the meeting with each person's needs named—raw material for a week's prayer.

Study 4. Psalm 8. Praying Our Creation.

Purpose: To develop a sense of orientation as a creature of God, living in the creation of God.

General note. The Bible pays a great deal of attention to context, the environment in which we live out our lives. The comprehensive name for this environment is "creation." The identity question of our culture is "Who am I?" It is interesting to compare it to the first question put to Adam in the garden, *"Where* are you?" God, it seems, is more interested in our geography than our psychology. And geography is an aspect of creation.

Group discussion. Throughout this study encourage the group to go beyond immediately personal answers and to explore the views of our culture. What disorienting effects do our culture's idolatrous views of God and reductionist views of humanity have on us?

Question 1. Prayer keeps our attention on God, who is the comprehensive context of existence. Everything—creation and creatures—is gathered into this context and seen in the light of "your name."

Question 3. This question is designed to gauge an initial reaction to who we are in light of this psalm. The subsequent questions will go into more depth regarding how this psalm defines our humanity. Then question 11 brings us back to the question of how we need to alter our self-image.

Question 6. It has been common in Christian reflection on this psalm to connect *mindful* with the Incarnation.

Question 9. Environmentalists hostile to the Christian faith have often leveled the accusation that the Bible and Christians are responsible for the rapacious treatment of the land in contrast, for instance, to American Indians who have a mystical reverence for it. Explore the experiences of the group—do they feel implicated in this accusation?

Question 11. Some people think of themselves as "a little higher than the heavenly beings"; others think "a little lower than the beasts of the field." Both extremes need correction. We don't improve or correct our self-image by looking in the mirror or by introspective meditation, but by prayer. Encourage the use of this prayer as a means of bringing our self-image into conformity with our God-image.

Study 5. Psalm 51. Praying Our Sin.

Purpose: To realize the exact nature of what is wrong with us before God, and to discover in a personal way what sin is.

General note. Most of us carry enormous loads of guilt that have nothing to do with God—guilt that comes from not meeting other people's expectations, or taking too seriously criticisms that have nothing to do with who we really are. This psalm helps us focus on the real issues of sin.

Background. You might read 2 Samuel 11—12 before the study and briefly summarize what happened in order to provide the background for the psalm.

Question 1. You can sharpen the meaning of these sin words by developing a parallel list of synonyms that we commonly use to name what we are dissatisfied with: low self-esteem, bad self-image, hangups, not very smart, don't have enough money and so on. Look for ways to contrast what God thinks of us with what we think of ourselves.

Question 3. If we are always trying to make ourselves more acceptable to ourselves and others, we are in a lifelong bondage to shifting opinions and standards we can never meet. If we are open to what God will do for our sin, we enter into spacious freedom, for we are no longer in charge of making ourselves better, but letting him make us holy.

Question 4. The question intends to develop an awareness of the broken relationship between us and God, which remains broken even when our behavior is respectable.

Question 6. God not only forgives us, cleansing us from the guilt of sin (vv. 1-9), he renews us, creating a pure heart within us (v. 10). Christians refer to these two aspects of salvation as *justification* and *sanctification*.

Question 11. It is almost inevitable that someone will begin making resolutions not to do "this" or "that" anymore. If they do, challenge them: the whole point of the psalm and the Christian gospel is that we can't do anything about our sin except confess it, and then submit to God's way of doing something about it.

Prayer. Be sure to allow a time of silence for group members to do this. It is an important part of the application of this passage.

Study 6. Psalm 103. Praying Our Salvation.

Purpose: To enter into the wealth of detail that is gathered into the act of salvation by praying Psalm 103.

General note. When salvation is reduced by sloganeering into a password, it is banalized. Salvation is not a step-by-step procedure to go through but a vast country to explore. Prayer is the means for doing this, and Psalm 103 is an excellent guidebook.

Group discussion. Encourage people to elaborate the details of whatever "best thing" is held up, but don't let the examples get separated into sacred and secular piles. Salvation is sacred, but it has the power to gather everything else into it.

Question 1. Be leisurely with this. There are no right and wrong answers. Talk about what you observe in the themes and language and how you feel as you read this.

Question 2. The *NIV Study Bible* notes that "O my soul" is "a conventional Hebrew way of addressing oneself." Also, the term *soul* is "Not a spiritual aspect in distinction from the physical, nor the psalmist's 'inner' being in distinction from his 'outer' being, but his very self as a living conscious, personal being" (pp. 887, 784).

Question 3. Note that "redeems" is a synonym for "delivers" (*NIV Study Bible,* p. 867).

Question 6. In your discussion of this question pay special attention to verses 11-14. The statements about heaven and earth, east and west, and a father and his children are incredibly rich in meaning.

Question 8. In order to get the full impact of these verses, encourage the group to use their imagination. Try to picture the mighty angels in one section of the orchestra, the heavenly hosts (countless multitudes) in another, all other created beings and things in another, and the psalmist standing in the conductor's place. With sweeping gestures, he draws out notes of praise first from one section then another, until the entire creation—including the psalmist—is praising and worshiping the Lord. This is an overpowering scene!

If no one else mentions it, point out that each member of the orchestra is characterized by obedience. The mighty ones *do his bidding* and *obey his word* (v. 20). The heavenly hosts are *servants* who *do his will* (v. 21). All his works are under *his dominion*. The assumption is that the psalmist and those whom the Lord has saved are also obedient to him.

Question 9. This might be the right time to have persons in the group share their own stories of salvation. As these stories are told, an alert leader can "footnote" the stories with phrases from the psalm or items from the earlier discussion.

Question 10. The assumption in the study questions is that everyone in the group is "saved." That, of course, may not be so. Invite the "unsaved" to tell their stories also: What do you think of all this? How do you feel when the rest of us are talking this way?

Study 7. Psalm 23. Praying Our Fear.

Purpose: To name and then pray the fears that are in our lives.

Group discussion. Everybody has fears, but the culture trains us to bluff our way through them. Our psychologized age names fears "phobias" and makes them evidence of neurosis. But the world *is* a fearful place. There is much to fear, both inside us and outside us. The healthiest thing to do with fear is to name it and then pray it. Our purpose in doing this is to discover God's presence in the experience of fear.

Some fears are based in reality, and some in fantasy. Fears based in reality serve to keep us alive a little longer; fears based in fantasy restrict the scope of our lives. Talk about the differences.

Question 1. If no one else mentions it, you might point out how many times personal pronouns (*I, me, my*) occur in the psalm. It is very personal! Did the group notice that the psalm is divided into two halves, each based on a different metaphor (see question 3)? You can encourage careful observation by naming all the metaphors, counting nouns, listing verbs, noting contrasts. But only do this if the group isn't getting anywhere on its own.

Question 4. The shepherd carried a rod (small club) for protection. His staff, which was longer and often curved at the end, was used primarily to guide and direct the sheep.

Question 5. For a sheep the "paths of righteousness" simply meant the right paths on which the shepherd guided him (although for us they have moral overtones). Therefore, when the sheep walks through the valley of the shadow of death (v. 4), it is not by accident—the shepherd has led him there and will protect him. You may have to make some distinctions here: "fearing no evil" is not the same thing as never having bad things happen to us. Prayer is not a rabbit's foot that wards off bad luck.

Question 6. The law of the desert was hospitality. If someone was running from an enemy and took refuge in a Bedouin tent, the hospitality could not be violated. That custom is implicit in the psalm. Hosts would sometimes anoint the heads of their guests with perfumed oil as a gesture of hospitality. The overflowing cup was a sign of the abundant provisions of the banquet.

Questions 8-10. Return to the discussion that came out of the earlier group discussion, and review what was said. Guide the group to responsibly deal with fears that are actually in their lives; don't wander off in conjecture about "what if."

Study 8. Psalm 137. Praying Our Hate.

Purpose: To learn first to admit and then to pray our hate.

General note. This may be the most difficult study in the series, but it is very important. If we don't learn to do what the psalmists did, facing and speaking the very worst that is inside us, our lives of prayer will never reach bedrock.

Question 1. It is easiest to begin with childhood experiences: hating parents for punishing us or making us do something we disliked; hating the neighborhood bully; hating an awful teacher. As we become "socialized" we learn not to use that language. But the experiences and feelings continue, often unadmitted. Until we bring them to the surface, they are not available for prayer.

Question 3. The experience of homesickness expressed here is one that is common to us. Sometimes it is evidence of loyalty. Sometimes it is simply irresponsibility. According to Leslie C. Allen:

Their grief was much more than homesickness. As they sat in an attitude of mourning beside a tree-lined canal, they were haunted by memories of Zion. They were the bittersweet memories of festivals and fellowship with God and with believer, and the tortured memories of the ruins to which God's earthly home and the capital of his realm had been reduced. Their lyres, once used to accompany God's glad praises, rested up in the branches, idle, silent. Tauntingly, their enemies bid them sing one of the old Songs of Zion. (*Psalms 101-150* [Dallas, Tex.: Word, 1983], p. 241)

Question 4. Israel had turned away from God, and God had allowed the Babylonians (Edomites) to take over Jerusalem and capture the Israelites in order to call them back to himself. If you think it's unlikely that anyone would know the historical background, you might fill it in yourself and then repeat the second part of the question.

Question 6. Verses 7-9 are bone-chilling. This is raw hate. It is also prayer.

Question 8. Remind the group that the psalmist wants the Babylonians to experience the same atrocities they had inflicted on Israel (notice v. 8). We need to realize that parents in Israel had to watch their infants being dashed against the rocks! The horror of this does not make their hatred acceptable, but it does make it more understandable.

Question 9. If you don't have any named enemies, you can't pray for them. Recall the discussion of question 8 in the previous study (on Psalm 23). Encourage the group to make their enemy list their prayer list.

Question 10. We could, by using this prayer, end up "hating on our knees," and justifying our hate by our posture. But this psalm is embedded in a collection of prayers that trains us in confession and praise. Psalm 137 is not a stopping place; we have to go on to Psalm 138 and 139 if we are going to grow in prayer.

Study 9. Psalm 6. Praying Our Tears.

Purpose: To learn to bring emotions into the act of prayer, not sentimentally but biologically.

General note. The task of prayer is to bring everything we are and feel before God. Emotions are tricky. They are a *fact* of our lives, but they easily become fraudulent. Prayer keeps them honest—*if* we pray them. Sorrow is a fact of life, but difficult to distinguish from self-pity. Psalm 6 helps to make the distinction and to cultivate the sorrow.

Personal reflection. If you have a fairly high level of comfort with one another, you may want to discuss this question as well. Pay attention to the causes of the weeping, the source of the tears. Some weeping is manipulative, trying to get others to feel sorry for us. Some weeping is selfish, from not getting our own way. Some weeping is compassionate, a deep feeling for the suffering in others. Don't be critical of anything that is expressed, but keep it in mind for later development.

Question 3. Explore why David would assume that the difficulties in his life—at least in part—were a result of the Lord's anger. This was a prayer prayed in a time of illness, "an occasion seized upon by David's enemies to vent their animosity." "Though the Lord has sent him illness to chastise him for his sin (see 32:3-5; 38:1-8, 17-18), the psalmist asks that God would not in anger impose the full measure of the penalty for sin, for then death must come (see v. 5; see also 130:3)" (*NIV Study Bible*, p. 784).

Question 8. There have been times in the history of faith when tears have been evidence of a deep life in Christ, feeling his agony on the cross and his weeping over Jerusalem, and participating in it. Our culture emphasizes the opposite: the happy Christian and the have-it-altogether saint. Are we missing something? Probe the discussion for signs of healthy tears: tears that arise from loss (bereavement, separation), tears that arise from repentance (something wrong with me) or compassion (something wrong in others). All other tears are probably either immature (childish) or wrong (sinful).

Study 10. Psalm 73. Praying Our Doubt.

Purpose: To bring doubt into the act of prayer by reflecting on Psalm 73.

General note. It is always a mistake to deny doubt or suppress it. But what else is there to do with it? It can't be ignored, for it unnerves and unsettles us. The biblical way is to *pray* doubt, and Psalm 73 shows us how.

Group discussion. One way to deal with doubts is to charge them head on with a cannonade of arguments. Such assaults are sometimes helpful, but many people are merely intimidated and decide to keep their doubts quietly to themselves. If voicing a doubt makes us liable to attack, we are going to be cautious about speaking up. So you might have to provide some reassurance here to encourage discussion.

Question 2. Doubt arises when there is a discrepancy between what we think should happen when God is in charge and what in fact we see happening. Get as much illustrative material from the group as you can decently manage.

Question 5. Worship is not argument. It is attending to the invisible because we believe that the quiet God we can't see is more solid and dynamic than the noisily arrogant people we can see. The practice of worship doesn't explain evil; it puts it in perspective. And it doesn't cure doubt but uses it as fuel to pray more ardently.

Question 8. It is clear how we are "supposed to" answer this question, but encourage honesty here. Wickness may be vivid to use because it is so clearly and frequently portrayed in the media.

Questions 10-11. It is important to lead the discussion in such a way that worship is understood as what we *do*, not what we *feel*. Worship is an orienting act in which we decide to let our lives be shaped by God instead of doing the best we can against whatever makes life difficult for us. It develops habitual faith (with doubts nagging at the edges) in contrast to habitual doubt (with faith nagging at the edges).

Study 11. Psalm 90. Praying Our Death.

Purpose: To come to grips with our mortality by facing the fact that we are going to die—maybe sooner, maybe later than we think—and to do so by praying Psalm 90.

General note. There is no particular virtue in simply thinking about death. It can be neurotic morbidity. But there is a Christian way to face death that sharply defines and sanely develops our dependence on and trust in God.

Group discussion. What is said and felt at funerals sometimes reveals our attitudes to death. If the group needs additional prompting with this question, ask follow-up questions such as: How do you feel at a funeral? What do you say to people who are bereaved? What has been your experience with the dying? Do you avoid them? Are you overly cheery?

Question 2. At the end of our lives, there is God. Death forces us, rather dramatically, to remember God. Some medieval monks slept in their coffins every night to keep themselves aware of the limits to their strength and the limitlessness of God's mercy. Does that appeal to you?

Questions 5-6. The biblical writers don't hesitate to use human words to describe the nature and action of God. This lack of caution is a great boon; there is nothing bloodless or abstract in the biblical God. But it also sets a difficult task for our imaginations. We must discriminate carefully what is meant, or we will end up with a picture of God which is only our own self enlarged. The "anger" of God requires interpretation. In one sense, God is not angry the way we are angry—flying off the handle because he is frustrated. But in another sense, our experience of anger tells something profound about God. Explore what it is.

The NIV Study Bible has a text note on Psalm 2:5 which says "God's anger is always an expression of his righteousness" (p. 781).

Question 11. The crucifixion death of Jesus is obviously the best example of preparing for a good death. Christians learn how to die by observing how Jesus died and by participating in it. The pattern set for us is not stoical but redemptive.

Study 12. Psalm 150. Praying Our Praise.

Purpose: To realize the comprehensiveness of praise and to set as a personal goal that all our prayers will eventually end up in praise.

General note. Prayer almost never begins in praise (it usually begins in hurt), but if pursued long enough, it will finally develop into praise. This doesn't mean that every prayer we make is capped off with praise, but that the life of prayer itself is always reaching toward praise. Most of the prayers in the Psalter, our training book in prayer, are not praises but laments. But they all end up at Psalm 150, praising the Lord. If we persist in prayer, we also will end up at Psalm 150, praising.

Group discussion. Make this a fun time. Play some appropriate festive music while you work. If possible, keep your praises on display for a few weeks.

Question 1. The Psalter is arranged into five books: 1—41, 42—72, 73—89, 90—106, 107—150. As preparation for this study, turn to the last psalm in each of the books and note its concluding verse. This "sense of an ending" gathers momentum through the Psalter.

Psalm 150 is not, by itself, the conclusion of Psalms. There are five "hallelujah" psalms, one for each book of the Psalter. These gather all the prayers offered in Israel and the church into praise. In order to see Psalm

150 in context, you may wish to observe a few of the complementary emphases in these five psalms (146—150).

Question 2. This study is organized around the following outline: *where* to praise the Lord (v. 1), *why* to praise him (v. 2), *how* to praise him (vv. 3-5) and *who* should praise him (v. 6). Various questions in the study point out this outline. However, if your group is more advanced you may wish to begin question 3 by asking: "What brief outline would you give to this psalm?" or "How would you divide this psalm into sections, and what brief title would you give to each one?"

The phrase "in his sanctuary" has been understood in various ways. Some commentators believe it is synonymous with "in his mighty heavens." If so, then it refers to God's dwelling place. Others believe it is a reference to the temple, God's earthly sanctuary, in contrast to "in his mighty heavens," his heavenly sanctuary. If so, then the psalmist is calling both earthly and heavenly worshipers to praise the Lord. If the group has difficulty answering this question, you might mention these possibilities and ask which one they feel best fits the context of the psalm.

Question 4. Encourage the group to imagine they are present at this worship service. What would they see and hear? What mood would fill the air? Then encourage them to compare this with their own corporate worship experience. What elements of worship in this psalm would they like to incorporate into their own worship?

Question 5. Look hard at the exceptions. Jesus on the cross is the biggest exception—how did that give praise?

Question 6. Guard against glibness here. It is easy to talk about what we "should" do in praising God and being grateful for what we have and are. But it is a lifelong assignment, not a weekend job.

Prayer. If you have time, you may wish to briefly review the different kinds of prayer that have been studied so far. Take the experience of each psalm (except 1 and 2) and discuss how those experiences can eventually become praise (or maybe already have for some people in the group). But don't rush it. It may take many years before some of these prayers "arrive" at Psalm 150.

Eugene H. Peterson, now retired, translated The Message *and wrote many books, including* A Long Obedience in the Same Direction *and the companion Bible study* Perseverance.